MW00760006

am I

Dave Waldrop
&
Lillie Clayton Waldrop Pannell

Printed in the United States of America.

ISBN-13: 978-0-9765700-2-8
ISBN-10: 0-9765700-2-5
Library of Congress Control Number: 2005906391

To order copies of *am I* or for information about Dave's spoken word CD, *Freedom*, contact Dave Waldrop at:
Dave Waldrop
PO Box 122
Webster, NC 28788
Tel: 828-586-6837
Email: dewaldrop@verizon.net

Editor: Michael Revere
Cover Photograph: Nancy Minard
Cover Design/Layout: Lisa M. Fisher

PPS Publishing
www.ppspublishing.com

Dedicated to my wife Edna, my son Brad, my daugher Erica, and my granddaughter Ella.

Table of Contents

Dave Waldrop

Dave Waldrop was born at home on October 14, 1943 a few miles north of Sylva, North Carolina.

Dave attended elementary school in Jackson County and graduated from Sylva Webster High School in 1962. While attending school he had enjoyed swimming, track, football, baseball, and basketball. Despite a general lack of confidence and being almost legally blind in his left eye, sports provided a good escape from the turmoil at home.

After graduation from high school, Dave enlisted in the United States Navy attending boot camp and Boilerman School, then served aboard the USS Preston for three and a half years.

Upon being honorably discharged from the U.S. Navy, he returned to Sylva to reconcile with his dying father and determine what to do with his life. He worked one year at the paper mill, then attended Western Carolina University majoring in psychology.

A few years later Dave returned to WCU and earned his Masters degree in Counseling and Guidance. For the next thirty years Dave provided counseling and guidance service for several mountain counties. His special concern was to provide care for people who are blind or visually challenged. In additional to counseling, Dave has worked as a school bus driver, coached football, basketball, baseball, and softball, and served as an elementary school athletic director. Dave's poetry and essays have been published in various magazines and newspapers around the region. He designed and sold an original cross-stitch pattern to a major department store chain, and has been recorded as a BMI songwriter.

In 1967 Dave married Edna Sutton. They have been married for 37 years and have been blessed with two children and a granddaughter.

Lillie Clayton Waldrop Pannell

Lillie Emmaline Clayton was born on April 12, 1918 in Dillsboro, NC. She lived in a house on Montieth Cove at the place called "Sheep Cliff."

She attended Dillsboro Elementary School and graduated from Sylva Central High School. Through her parents and community she developed a deep devotion to God and her fellow human beings.

When Lillie was a senior in high school, she married a man from Franklin, NC, named Charles "Brad" Waldrop. They had seven children and for the next 24 years she dedicated her life to the task of holding the family together. She provided unconditional love and protection for her children from Brad's violent and unpredictable alcoholic behavior. The fact that she survived the brutality at all is a testament to her toughness, her steadfast reliance on God, and her commitment to her children.

Brad died of cirrhosis of the liver in 1966 at the age of 55. After his death Lillie entered the second phase of her life, which included a career change and the marriage to Jerald Lee Pannell.

She attended Western Carolina University and earned her degree in Early Childhood Education. After several years of teaching kindergarten, Lillie decided that she needed to become a Licensed Practical Nurse. She attended Southwestern Community College and upon graduation, worked at Harris Regional Hospital for the next twenty years. After her retirement from Harris Regional Hospital, she continued to work two days a week as a children's therapeutic clown.

On October 14, 1994, at the age of 77, Lillie suffered a massive stroke. She was unable to speak nor had the ability to use her right arm and right leg. She lived in a rest home until her death on August 19, 2001.

Lillie's poems appear in this book to honor and pay homage to this courageous and loving mountain woman. These precious poems are a way to see inside her soul, offering hope and inspiration to her fellow human beings.

Acknowledgments

Some of these poems and lyrics appeared in the following publications and CD:

Asheville Citizen Times

Cheorkee One Feather

Southwestern Community College Art &
  Literature Magazine, Milestone

The Smoky Mountain Boys
  CD (Victory is Coming)

am I

you say you saw it on the evenin' news
you said man that just ain't right.
them kids was killin' each other
and it was out in the broad daylight

you say those are the children
ain't no fortunate ones.
ain't goin' no long distance
no long run.

but it's the land of the brave
it's the home of the free.
are you gonna judge me
by what you see on your t.v.?

and you say you've been sittin' there thinkin'
just wonderin' 'bout them kids.
are they ever gonna be forgiven
for the things they did?

and who is to bless and who'll bear the blame
and who are the guilty?
and where in the world is the shame?
in the land of the brave
and the home of the free.

are you gonna judge me
by what you see on your t.v.?

and for the support of this declaration,
with a firm reliance on the protection of divine Providence,
we mutually pledge to each other our lives,
our fortunes and our sacred honor.

and the cloth said billy, you're a might fine boy.
if you stick with me there'll be a lot of joy.
and the teacher said johnny—so welcome at school.
but if you ain't goin' to college how you gonna be cool?
and bobby's lookin' for his daddy in the numbers books.
but he may never find him no matter how hard he looks.

but it's the land of the brave
and the home of the free.
are you gonna judge me
by what you see on your t.v.?

am i my brother's keeper? am i my brother's keeper?
am i my brother's keeper? am i my brother's keeper?
am i ?

Momma

We know you as Momma as all children should.

We see you as a symbol of everything that's good.

None of us remember when you didn't shower love.

For you had that endless supply from the good Love up above.

Friends and neighbors still tell us of things you did for them—

A giver, not a taker, devoted to every woman and man.

You had seven children who came forth by birth

and felt what you gave all—the Almighty's sense of worth.

We watched you be a daughter, a sister, and a wife.

We thank you for being there as a model for our lives.

Thank you, Momma! Thank you, Momma! Thank you!

Thank you, Momma! Thank you, Momma! Thank you!

Lillie Clayton Waldrop Pannell

Life's Way

My Trial

Today I had a trial,
I don't know why 'twas sent.
It must have been a lesson,
and to help me it was meant.

The customers got on my nerves
their speech gave me the jitters.
It must have been a test
to see if I were a quitter.

I would try to think just how to act
and be mindful of my manners,
when they would try to taunt
and show their ugly banners.

There is something to annoy and vex
the very best of men.
If all this should cease to be,
I suppose our life would end.

My Book of Memories

I have a book of memories
of pages sweet and clear.
Of the days and nights I've spent
With those I love so dear.

First, here's a page of little boys
bringing many tears and joys.
Sister comes to change the scene
and it's books and babysitting in between.

Now some have made good marks in school
and learned to live the Golden Rule
May they strive to be of service to others
just as all true sisters and brothers.

Home

What is home to you my friend
at the ending of the day?
Just somewhere to go and snatch a bite
and then be on your way?

Or is it a rest of love and quiet
with loved ones 'round about?
The welcome fire on a wintry night
when it's cold and dark without.

A home where mother's pleasant smile
the cares of life erase,
and dear old Dad is waiting there
to brighten up the place?

Let's turn again to love and home
and help our children see,
just what a wonderful place
a happy home can be!

My Neighbors

I can see her now as she approached the door
And greeted me in days of yore.
She was wearing a print dress and apron neat
And spoke in a voice so tender and sweet.

She would ask me in to sit a spell
And all the news we would tell.
She would never slander or tell a lie
And was always considerate of everyone nigh.

Her house was always cozy and neat
And for cleanliness she couldn't be beat.
The beds were made in sheets so white
And the windows covered with curtains bright.

The fire upon the hearth was aglow,
With flickers dancing to and fro.
Made you feel a welcome there
Of the old-fashioned love of this pair.

The little cookstove on the kitchen side
Where, hardly ever the fire died

Was always ready to cook a meal
That to any king would appeal.

The kettle sang a merry song
And no sorrow could last for long.
For this was a house where love dwelt.
The lasting kind that could be felt.

Lord, help me to have such a home
Where ever upon this earth I may roam.
Til someone someday may say
She helped me to find a better way.

"Can't" and "Can"

"Can't" lives in a house of gloom
with dark pictures hanging in every room.
The cobwebs hang from the ceilings there
and all the shelves are empty and bare.

Yet, "can" lives in a garden fair
where there is beauty beyond compare.
The birds are singing a happy song
and flowers are blooming from dawn to dawn.

The sky is the ceiling
the Earth is the floor…
how could anyone ask
for more?

Who will you choose as your friend…
and in whose place will you your days spend…
in the house of "Can't" or the world of "Can"?
each choice determines the kind of man.

Town on Saturday

Do you ever go to town
on a Saturday
to see the different sights
and pass the time away?

There's a happy vendor
selling his "popcorn"
and over there's a little boy
blowing on his horn.

I don't know how t'would be
with no place to "gad" around
so I'm glad there's still
the little country town.

Patience

One day I asked for patience
and much to my surprise,
the next thing I knew
tears had filled my eyes.

For I had failed my test
and everything went wrong.
Just about now—I noticed
patience came along.

We learn to be patient
by suffering adversity,
and by not getting so upset
when things don't go so easy.

We must know some sorrow
to see true happiness,
and sometimes a taste of failure
before a great success.

The Day of Small Things

Do you have just a little brain?
Well, use it and more knowledge you will gain
to live a life of usefulness
and of far greater happiness.

Do you have just a little abode?
Only a cottage beside the road?
Then make it a castle that is happy and gay;
help some pilgrim along life's way.

Do you have just a little town?
Build it up…don't let it down.
Live a life that's pure and clean.
Shun all that is evil and mean.

What if the little acorn should say,
"I'll never be anything anyway.…
No tree with branches wide and high,
So, I'll just lie here until I die."

No, this is not just the Maker's Plan
each must do the best he can.
And use each talent large or small
and grow like that giant oak—strong and tall.

Strength

Sometimes I feel cheated, sometimes mistreated.
Sometimes I feel like a fool.
Sometimes I feel disgusted, sometimes get busted
'cause I don't always play the rules.
Sometimes I feel rejected, sometimes detected
for something that some thing is wrong.
Sometimes I feel defeated, but my life ain't completed
till I've sung all my outlaw songs.

Sometimes I feel like quitting, sometimes like spitting
for places I've never been.
Sometimes I feel like staying, simply delaying
till I've tasted my share of sin.
Sometimes I feel dismayed, sometimes betrayed
by the feelings I place on the line.
I'm seeking refuge from trouble and abuse,
but I keep ongoing one day at a time.

Sometimes I seek treasure, sometimes share pleasure
with someone who's looking for love.
Sometimes I feel run down, sometimes wear a frown.
Then I stop and thank God above

for giving me strength to go the full length

in a life that's different each day.

Till I breathe my last breath on the threshold of death

I hope I can always say

I'm an outlaw, a cowboy, and a misfit for sure.

I feel more like I do now that I did before.

Woodpecker

Well, the red-headed woodpecker peckin' in a tree
ain't doin' no harm to you and me.
He's just getting' him somethin' to eat
usin' that lightnin' powerful beak.

Now, I like the sound that the woodpecker makes
except when he pecks my cedar shakes.
So, I leave him a dead tree or two
for somethin' to eat and somethin' to do.

You know—the red-headed woodpecker used to be plenty.
Nowadays we ain't got too many.
So, we better start doin' everything we can
to keep what God put on this land.

Now, the red-headed woodpecker doin' no harm
peckin' in your trees or peckin' on your barn.
She's just doin' the best she can
to live in harmony with man.

Jesus Loves You

Sometimes you're up; sometimes you're down.
Sometimes you forget that Jesus is around
Sometimes it seems that your whole world turns blue.
But, don't you forget that Jesus loves you.

Yes, Jesus loves you. Yes, Jesus loves you.
Yes, Jesus loves you and He always will.

Darius threw Daniel into the lion's den
Because he worshipped the true God—not him.
Jesus saved Daniel—I know that is true.
What He did for Daniel He'll do for you.

I knew a man who had troubles everywhere.
Sometimes he told me "Jesus just don't care."
But, just when it seemed that all his hope was gone
You know what happened—Jesus came along.

Yes Jesus loves you. Yes, Jesus loves you.
Yes Jesus loves you and He always will.

1861

They called us young boys off to that war
without fully explaining what we were fighting for
except that there was a war and we had to fight.
They told us there was a war and we had to fight.

'Cause the North was a strangling the South they said.
Yet, men could be bought for $500 a head
and the war would show everybody who was wrong and right.
They said the war would show everybody who was wrong and right.

So we fought at Bull Run, Antietam, too.
And down at Vicksburg we lost quite a few.
Though the generals kept telling us—Boys, we're winning this thing.
Yeah, the generals kept telling us—Boys, we're winning this thing.

But, we kept dreaming about our farms
and wondering why we'd ever taken up arms
back in '61—What a beautiful spring.
I remember '61 was a beautiful spring.

And Joseph dreamed a dream, and he told it his brethren:
and they hated him yet the more.
And Joseph dreamed a dream, and he told it his brethren:
and they hated him yet the more.

Then Lincoln freed the people at Gettysburg.
General Lee surrendered. Have you heard?
And that awful, bloody war started coming to an end.
Yeah, that awful, bloody war started coming to an end.

But, too many thousand who had worn blue and gray
are calling to us, still, from cold, cold graves
saying—Nobody ever needs to go through that again.
They're saying—Nobody ever needs to go through that again.

And, we hold these truths to be self-evident—
Do we hold these truths to be self-evident?

American Workers

We may try to strip them of their pride.
With ignorance and arrogance we have glorified
people who push papers and sign the big contracts.
But, we always wind up ridin' on workin' folks' backs.

Let's give workin' folks their overdues
for the houses, buildings, bridges, and the energy we use.
Let's give praises to the spirit that these folks so freely give
to make America the best place in the world to live.

Let's tip our hats to the American workin' woman and man.
They deserve respect, though they seldom demand.
Most call them blue collar. Their wages ain't top dollar.
But, they're always the backbone of this great land.

Ballet on the Lake

The ballet on the lake began. I watched with gratitude

for the way God speaks to us about our attitudes.

We drift like boats on water from the things that we should do.

But when the lightning flashes we wonder—are we true?

The thunder rocks things 'round us—we seek that firm Refuge

from the mighty raging storms that are bound for me and you.

No one can stop the rain. The fire ball always shines.

Along with joy we will have pain. God gives everything its time.

The air we breathe we cannot make though

some would claim they can.

And the water for the stage cannot be made by man.

I am grateful for this ballet—the stage so beautifully set.

It's such a simple pleasure, but the beauty I won't forget.

My Feet

My feet are made for walking,
not just for standing still.
My feet are made for running.
You can bet they will.
They give my body freedom
to go from place to place
but wherever they may take me
my feet will leave a trace—
A trace that can be followed
right back to their start,
and Mom and Dad
know where that is.
It's inside their hearts.

Martin Luther King, Jr.

He lived his life in troubled times
and worked to the tune of his church's chimes.
He conducted his mission in a positive way
with little regard to monetary pay.
He believed in equality for all people.
His campaign worked outward from the steeple.
His belief was strong and his courage great.
He had a dream that could not wait.
He spent his life working on that dream
so his brothers and sisters could join the team.
Though Martin is dead his spirit remains.
Let's make it a point to remember his name.

Daddy

on 10/14/43 i was born the 6th son
of an alcoholic paper mill worker
and a devout christian housewife
with one older half sister and one younger sister
22 years later my daddy died with cirrhosis of the liver

he would not let us study at home
he never told me he loved me
he beat my mother repeatedly
he held us at gunpoint quite often
he systematically isolated us from the community and our relatives
he separated us from each other within the family
he told us we were stupid
we moved 19 times in 18 years (sometimes as a family;
sometimes just a few to escape the mental/physical cruelty)
he never provided for our half sister/never introduced us to her
three of my brothers and my younger sister left home
before finishing high school
he claimed a particular contempt for baptist preachers

i thought we were the only family in the world
who survived like we did
i thought everybody knew what it was like in our house
sometimes i thought we were the reason he drank

when he was young he liked to fix cars, farm, fish, hunt, play guitar,

sing, dance—he gradually gave up all those things

i learned that all alcoholics are very intelligent

i learned that alcoholism is a disease

i learned that some are runners, some are stayers,

some are behavioral, some are physiological

he worked at the paper mill until he could no longer work safely

luckily for us they allowed him to retire

(today he would have been fired)

he paid all debts

he taught us not to lie

he taught us not to steal

he taught us we were better than no one

he told people at the mill what great kids he had

on the night of 10/04/66,

i bought him the last pint of liquor he ever saw

it was smarter to get it for him than to let him go and get robbed

that night my wonderful mother was in michigan

helping to bring a grandchild into this great world

i told him he would never finish that pint

he didnt

on the morning of 10/05/66, I found him dead was stiff

some of our neighbors sent him to hell
i just listened
i felt it would do no good to ask them not to judge
i do believe that he left his prison that night
the Eagles said "Your prison is walking through this world all alone."
he walked alone because he rejected his family, his Maker,
and then his family again
Bruce Springsteen said "When a man turns his back on his family
he just aint no good"

people will tell you that alcohol kills alcoholics
it dont
rejection does

i loved him then
i love him now
he is my daddy

Love is Perfect

Don't you know, people—we need love and kindness?
It won't take much—just a little of you.
Make someone's storm clouds roll away
and let the Son come shining through.

May come a time when you have a problem.
It can get rough walkin' down life's road.
It's nice to know there's always somebody
who will be glad to help you carry your load.

Go on! Show somebody you care.
Give a little bit of your love.
Show somebody you care.
Love is something this world needs more of.
Love is something we all need more of.

Through all the sunshine
through all the rain
love is a perfectly wonderful thing.

Kudzu

Kudzu grows on roadbanks
and up on power poles.
I don't know who brought it here, but, God rest their souls.
They brought it here
to keep the blessed soil from washin' away.
But, how could they know
that kudzu'd grow at least a foot a day?

Kudzu grows a foot a day
if it grows at all.
It can climb the highest tree,
up, or through a wall.
Don't sit too close to it
when you've got nothin' to do.
'Cause if you sit there for too long
Kudzu'll cover you.

There's miles and miles of Kudzu
down in Dixie land.
It grows well in water
and on any kind of land.
Now it's started to grow up North,
at least that's what they say.
So, the folks up there can sit and watch
it grow a foot a day.

Kudzu grows a foot a day
if it grows at all.
It can climb the highest tree,
up, or through a wall.
Don't sit too close to it
when you've got nothin' to do.
'Cause if you sit there for too long
Kudzu'll cover you.

You've heard of Jack's beanstalk.
Well, I'll tell you the truth.
Instead of a beanstalk
Jack set out Kudzu.
He set it out at suppertime
and then to sleep he lay.
It had grown up to the sky
by the break of day.

Kudzu grows a foot a day
if it grows at all.
It can climb the highest tree
up, or through a wall.
Don't set too close to it
when you've got nothin' to do.
'Cause if you sit there for too long
Kudzu'll cover you.

IV

Down through time people have been very curious about our origin. During my lifetime I have heard and read about creation by a living God as taught in the King James version of the Bible. I have also heard and read about the theory of evolution as developed by Charles Darwin in a book called *The Origin of Species*. I just finished reading a very scholarly book entitled *Evolution, Creationism, and Other Modern Myths* by Vine Deloria, Jr. Deloria points out that for centuries the debate and controversy have been between these two schools of thought—creation and evolution. He makes his point for the inclusion of catastgrophism as an explanation for the destruction of many species and the development of others. It seems, however, that for a while to come we will continue to polarize with the creation/evolution scenario.

This brings me to an observation which I have made while reading, listening, and thinking about our origin. According to Genesis I there are four fairly distinct categories of things that interact. Those four things are: time, God, resources, and people. When one looks at strict evolutionary thinking it becomes clear that under that thinking only two things exist.

They are: time and resources—living and non-living resources. According to evolution and creation man came last.

It's likely that other people have observed this comparison of evolution and creation. However, I have never read or heard of it. I just thought I would reveal what I have reasoned.

Back Home

I've made more than my share of mistakes
I must admit, and hung on to some habits
after all my friends said quit.
But somehow or another
I keep on keeping on
hoping that someday I'll find
a way to get back home.

I'd like to sit out on the porch
with my daddy one more time,
say yes sir when he said son,
one day at a time.
I'd go sit down at the table
with Momma when she called
and look up at the picture
she kept hanging on the wall.

Wolfe said—You can't go home again
I hope that's not true.
So many things left undone
that I'd sure to do.
Now somehow or another
I will keep on keeping on
And hoping that someday I find
a way to get back home.

The Woman I Love

Groundhog lives in a hole in the ground.
Squirrel lives in a tree.
Birds fly high up in the sky.
Fish swim deep in the sea.
These are a few of the things I like
that were made by God above.
But, the thing that He made
that I like the most
is the woman that I love.

Water runs downhill all the time.
The wind blows everywhere.
The sun shines warm up in the sky
to remind us that He cares.
These are a few of the things I like
that were made by God above.
But, the thing that He made
that I like the most
is the woman that I love.

I love the woman I love
though it can't be explained.
I love the woman I love.
She's the lifeblood in my veins.
I love the woman I love.
I love her all the time.
I love the woman I love
And I'm mighty proud to call her mine.

Teeny, Tiny Toe-Tapping Tadpole from Turtle Town, Tennessee

There was a teeny tiny toe-tapping tadpole
from Turtle Town, Tennessee.
And it seemed that he might've had
a mighty special message for you and me.
If you don't like the way that you look
just take a good look at me—
said the teeny, tiny, toe-tapping tadpole
from Turtle Town, Tennessee.

No! I don't like the way I look
now, nor the way I'm gonna be.
And I wonder if there's someone somewhere
who'd like to trade places with me.
And I wouldn't have to spend the rest
of my life just being little old me—
Teeny tiny, toe-tapping tadpole
from Turtle Town, Tennessee.

I'd like to be a person for a while.
How happy I would be.
I'd like to walk on my own two feet
and I'd make other people happy.
An' I'd wear a smile upon my face
for the rest of eternity
'cause I wasn't that teeny tiny, toe-tapping tadpole
from Turtle Town, Tennessee.

Steel Mill

In Weirton, West Virginia, there's a steel mill.
And workin' in that mill, Lord, it's hot enough to kill.
But, you know it ain't the heat or workin' on their feet
That's just about to break them people's will.

Are they really gonna shut the steel mill down?
What's gonna happen to the people in this town?
Ain't gonna be no peace of mind if them people find
out they're really gonna shut the steel mill down.

Fathers worked with their fathers and their sons
doin' all the things that they knew must be done.
You know that they can't hide their heartache or their pride
about the mill that they have built in Weirton.

Are they really gonna shut the steel mill down?
What's gonna happen to the people in this town?
Ain't gonna be no peace of mind if them people find
out they're really gonna shut the steel mill down.

Fraser Fir

Well, we took a little trip
up to Waterrock Knob.
And, I wasn't even thinkin'
'bout gettin' no job.
But, when I got there
What did I see?
I saw the skeletons
Of Fraser fir trees.

I asked myself—
What's goin' on
When a friend of mine
Can't sing his song?
Then I asked my Maker—
What can I do
To help the Fraser fir trees
Stay green and blue?

I've got me a job—
Doin' the best I can.
I'm beggin' you, lady.
I'm beggin' you, man—
Won't you find out
What you can do
To help the Fraser fir trees
Stay green and blue.

Pure Love (Back to Basics)

Some folks criticized Him for His company.
Some called Him the devil in disguise.
When He saw things that weren't worth keeping,
the fire could burn hot in His eyes.
But, His heart overflowed with pure love.
He stood fast in fightin' for His cause.
And the words that He told us in His teachings
Are much greater than the greatest of our laws.

Most people in His time misunderstood Him.
They thought He should be an earthly king,
but He turned down each offer that they gave Him
and just gave them the love He'd come to bring.
There's lots of trouble this old world is facin'
because of greed and want for earthly power.
And if we ever needed Divine Guidance,
God knows there's never been a darker hour.

We say we're getting back to the basics.
Well, let's get back to the truth of His word
and treat each other as Jesus taught us
in the greatest story ever heard.

One of the Fold

Wanderin' with no sense of direction
like a ship adrift on the sea—
a child with no home for protection
till Jesus' face I did see.
Then I prayed—Dear Jesus,
please save me!
Make me one of the fold.
Now I am going with Jesus
to the land where we'll never grow old.

I'm going where we'll never grow old
to the Land where we'll never grow old.
I'll live forever with Jesus
singing—Thank God! I'm one of the fold.

If you're tossed on a deep sea of trouble,
sinking in sin and despair,
don't you lose hope, my dear brother.
Just reach out. Jesus is there!
Pray—Jesus, dear Jesus, please save me.
Make me one of the fold.
In His loving arms He will take you
to the Land where we'll never grow old.

We're going where we'll never grow old—
to the Land where we'll never grow old.
We'll live forever with Jesus
singing—Thank God! We belong to the fold.

George Jones

Lord, I love White Lightnin'. It's one great country song.
Ever' time I hear George Jones I gotta sing along.
I've loved country music since the day that I was born.
Nobody gonna tell me—Turn down George Jones.

Hey, the Devil went down to Georgia—He stopped lovin' her today
Okie from Muskogee. What more need I say?
I've loved country music since the day that I was born.
Nobody gonna tell me—Turn down George Jones.

Play the Orange Blossom Special, Harper Valley P.T.A.
Take This Job and Shove It, and the Wildwood Flower, hey, hey.
I've loved country music since the day that I was born.
Nobody gonna tell me—Turn down George Jones.

Nobody gonna tell me—Turn down George Jones.
I've got that country music in my blood and in my bones.
If you don't like it, mister, mister, just move on.
Nobody gonna tell me—Turn down George Jones.

Out the Door

Somehow that woman made me feel better
than I've ever felt before.
Then she turned around and tore it all down
when she walked right out the door.
And I felt confused, even abused,
but I know that's not all true,
'cause she made my world as bright as a rainbow
just before she made it all blue.

Why she couldn't stay, why she called it a day
there's a chance that I'll never know.
But, love can't be shackled, tied up, or tackled.
She needed the freedom to go
searching for something or someone
wherever her spirit demands.
And I wish her well though it's been pure hell
without the touch of her hand.

Whether it's better to love and to lose
than to never love at all
right now there's no way that I can tell
'cause I haven't got up from the fall.

If time helps to heal this old broken heart
and I start to see my way through,
I'll say—she made my world as bright as a rainbow
just before she tore it apart.

She left me with the blues on my mind.
And a sad old, sad aching heart,
she put my world together
just before she tore it apart.

Livin' in Make-Believe

How come you treat me like this, woman?
How come you make me sad and blue?
How come you treat me like this, woman?
Lord, I love no one but you.

I had a dream late last night
That you were mine and mine alone.
But, I woke up to realize
You didn't even sleep at home.

My friends tell me I'm a fool
to keep livin' in make-believe.
Say as much as you stay gone
I oughta make you pack up and leave.

I do appreciate my friends
Though there's one thing they don't know.
If I could do without you, woman,
I'd done that a long time ago.

How come you treat me like this, woman?
How come you make me sad and blue?
How come you treat me like this, woman?
Lord, I love no one but you.

Kin to You

Where do we come from? Where do we go?

Most folks wonder. Maybe you know.

Are we born evil? Are we born good?

How can I give you the respect that I should?

And how can we learn all the things we should do?

Now, would you mind if I be kin to you?

What is the relationship really supposed to be

when it comes right down to you and me?

And how should we treat all the flora and the fauna?

How should we express time in our songs?

These are some things I've been wondering about

and I reckon I'll wonder till the time I check out.

Where do we come from? Where do we go?

Most folks wonder. Maybe you know.

Love Everybody

Can a Christian hate his brother 'cause he's black or white?
Can a Christian hate his sister 'cause she ain't livin' right?
Can a Christian hate his neighbor 'cause of what he's done?
No, I believe the Good Book tells us to love everyone.

So, love everybody, Christians. Jesus told us to.
Love everybody, Christians, though it's hard to do.
Love everybody, Christians, though they don't love you.
Love everybody, Christians. Jesus told us to.

Can a Christian turn his back on someone down and out?
Can a Christian not show others what Jesus is about?
Can a Christian hate the red yet love the yellow one?
No, I believe the Good Book tells us to love everyone.

So, love everyone, Christians. Jesus told us to.
Love everybody, Christians, though it's hard to do.
Love everybody, Christians, though they don't love you.
Love everybody, Christians. Jesus told us to.

The Cherokees

We have tried too hard to change the Cherokees.
Why could we not just let them be?
They were stewards of the land,
returning to its demand.
We have tried too hard to change the Cherokees.

They had a way of life that may be lost.
We may always have to pay the cost
for the people who were scattered
and the lives that we battered.
We have tried too hard to change the Cherokees.

Why don't we just try to love them?
God put no one above them.
He gave them what we call ours.
We say land belongs to powers.
We have tried too hard to change the Cherokees.

With great strength they have withstood us,
maybe never understood us
for thinking somehow we are better.
It is nowhere in His letters.
We have tried too hard to change the Cherokees.

The Cost

Ain't nothin' gonna stop me now
I'll get to the top somehow.
Been down so damned long
but I've always found the will to move on.
Changin' with the winds of time,
leavin' some good things behind.
Takin' the good with the bad,
seekin' things I never had.
goin' places I've never been,
turnin' strangers into my friends.
missin' some things I have lost.
Sometimes payin' a cost
that just don't seem fair.

But I'll pay a cost if
I'm going somewhere
And I'll pay a cost
even if I'm going nowhere.

So, I've got to keep moving on
looking for my place in the sun,
working for better days

sometimes getting no pay.
Not trying to be what I ain't—
half devil and half saint.
Holdin' on to what I can make.
Hopin' for one big break.
Countin' all the blessings He gave
for my voyage from cradle to grave,
Minimizing what I have lost—
most times paying the cost
that just doesn't seem fair.

But I'll pay a cost
If I'm going somewhere.
And I'll pay a cost
even if I'm going nowhere.

¾ Time

I've grown tired of livin' in ¾ time
shackled by limits of other men's minds—
followin' people whose eyes have turned blind.
From now on my life will be mostly mine.

I've missed out on some things I should have enjoyed,
filled up some spaces I should have left void—
been fun for some folks, I should have annoyed.
Might say I'm cuttin' my umbilical chord.

But I'll chart my own direction for the future,
live my life and somehow get along.
When I'm six feet under and made my last blunder
folks can say that fool just wrote his own song.

Steve Streater

Steve was good in all the sports—made the headlines and reports.
His handsome head was filled with dreams.
I cheered for him from the stands, felt a part of this great man
as he helped to build my favorite teams.
He set records on the mound that may never tumble down,
but the records they're just memories for him now.
You see his sails have been torn by a mighty raging storm.
But Steve's gonna sail again I know someway, somehow
'cause there ain't no way to keep a good man down.

Sometimes sits in his wheelchair wondering who really cares—
Seems like he could count them on this toes.
Then he looks up in the sky and he sees you and I—
Then more than the blades of grass that grow.
He set records on the mound that may never tumble down,
but the records they're just memories for him now.
You see his sails have been torn by a mighty raging storm.
But Steve's gonna sail again I know someway, somehow
cause there ain't no way to keep a good man down.

Sleepin' With My Darlin'

The bright lights called me to the city.
I left her in our old hometown.
I should have got a job in a circus.
I would have made a perfect clown.

Why she took me back I'll never know.
But, I'm mighty glad that she could.
I think she knows how sad I've been.
I think she knows I'm back for good.

And, tonight I'm sleepin' with my darlin'.
Her heart beats softly in my ears.
I will never leave her again.
She will never again cry lonesome tears.

Prayer

Father, forgive us for what we do
that we know we ought not.
Father, forgive us for what we don't do
that we know well that we ought.
Help us to see Thy will for our lives—
Then to do Thy will.
Then remind us that though we do fail
Thy love abides still.
Help us to be more forgiving with others
than we often want to be.
Help us to seek, Lord, not earthly things
but closer devotion to Thee.
Amen

No Nukes

Can't lay down and sleep at night
worrying 'bout the big bomb threat.
I don't know of anything worse
that's been invented yet.

The leaders keep buildin' up arsenals
and gettin' all ready to fight.
And if some fool should pull the handle
who'll know who was wrong and right?

You could take all the people in the world
who want a nuclear war
and put 'em in the parkin' lot
at Bradley's general store.
Why can't all the leaders see
there'll be no victory
if somebody drops the big bomb
on mankind's history.

No nukes needed in the USA
and Russia and China, too.
We got to have a place to live
for people like me and you.

Harry Chapin

Knew you as a singer,
a writer in your time.
What you wrote and sang about
did penetrate our minds—
songs for the folks who have a load
too great to carry.
So I had to sing this song
for you, Harry.

You sang about the love
between a father and a son
and all the things they didn't do
and all they should have done.
And though your time has come and gone
the songs will always carry
a special message for this world.
Thank you, Harry.

You gave your talents to this world,
hoped for truth and love.
I know you're listenin' to this song
somewhere up above.
And while I'm talkin' to you
I ain't gonna tarry
'cause I want you to know
we love you, Harry.

God's Gift

Daddy took to drinkin' way 'fore I was born.
When I asked my mom about it
she said—son, that's just the thorns.
You're bound to find some roses as you travel on
and sometimes you will find them in the words of a song.
Just hold on to Jesus. He will not let you down.
Then she taught me Amazing Grace—Lord how sweet the sound.

When my daughter asked me—daddy, what's ozone?
I said—honey, don't you worry. You'll never walk alone.
Just put your trust in Jesus as you travel on.
Remember what grandma told us with her songs.
Jesus is the only one who will not let us down.
Then I taught her Amazing Grace—Lord how sweet the sound.

Amazing Grace—sweetest song I ever heard.
Amazing Grace—oh, what beautiful words.
Amazing Grace—it's for all, not just a few.
Amazing Grace—God's gift to me and you.

Place and Time

I've often wished that I could have lived
in another place or time,
cause sometimes I can't seem to fit where I'm at—
at least not in my mind.
If I could change my circumstances
I'm not really sure I would
cause I might be tradin' for somethin' that's worse
than somethin' that's basically good.

We can dream of cowboys out on the range
or conquest in outer space.
We can sit and dream of the changes
and try to control the pace.
We can be cowboys in outer space
or spacemen in cowboy suits
or just sit and wonder whether to carry
lasers or wear cowboy boots.

If I could stop time I'd just stop myself,
and, God knows I can't do that.
If I could stop changes I'd stop this whole world
and someone would lay us down flat.

So I'll keep changin' with the world and the times,
doin' the best that I can
and prayin' that when I'm layin' down flat
I'll be described as a man.

The haves are still havin'; the have nots still nottin'.
Some people swear that this whole world is rotten.
But, it's a good place, the best that I've been.
If I could leave here alive I'd come back again.

Remember

Do you remember when you were a child
and could let your innocent dreams run wild?
What you dreamed of was—love don't fade away.
Remember how you hoped and prayed
that somehow, somewhere, someday
you'd find true love and you'd make true love stay.

Do you remember that you said I do—
when the preacher man said—Son, do you
take this beautiful woman to be your wife?
Do you remember that you said—I do—
when the preacher man said—Son, do you
believe this love should last for life?

Do you remember when the preacher man said
Will you take this man's hand
and promise him your love through joy and sorrow.
Do you remember when the preacher man said
Will you take this man
and promise him all of your tomorrows.

Hold on to your hopes and dreams.
Don't ever let true love fade away.

North Georgia Saturday Night

Way up in north Georgia
under the Blue Ridge sky
we still got enough Mother Nature
to make us country folks high.
We get under the moonshine
long 'bout Saturday night,
start playing sweet country music
and folks start feeling right.
It's good times on the mountain
on a north Georgia Saturday night.

Jimbo plays the guitar
kinda like Johnny Be Good.
Lester gets down on that fiddle
like old C.D. should.
John Boy plays that 'lectric bass
like no one else in sight.
We start playing sweet country music
and folks start feeling right.
It's good times on the mountain
on a north Georgia Saturday night.

Freedom

I am your National symbol.
That's something I'm so proud to say.
But, once on that brink of extinction
I feared I might have to say—
So long to America—
once the land of the brave and the free.
The freedom that I symbolize for you
you'd made so fragile for me.

I am the Bald-headed Eagle
still soarin' up in your skies.
I hope you'll look up and see me.
I hope you'll hear me cry—
Hello, my America—
still the land of the brave and the free.
The freedom that I symbolize for you
you have assured for me.

The freedom that I symbolize for you
you must assure for me.

Hallelujah

You know Jesus spent some time on this old world below
tryin' to teach us what we need to know.
For our salvation He died on Calvary.
And, I want to thank Him for what He's done for me.

Sometimes your troubles seem too hard to bear.
That's when you need to go to God in prayer.
He will rescue you from the ragin' storm.
With His love He will keep you safe and warm.

I wanna sing sing sing sing halleluja hallelujah.
I wanna sing sing sing sing halleluja hallelujah.
I wanna s i n g sing halleluja hallelujah.
And give praises and give praises to my Lord.

Keep Holdin' On

When your back's against the wall
you think you've seen it all,
when you've walked your last mile
and smiled your last smile.

When you're feelin' down and out
wonderin' what your life's about,
Your old friends don't come around;
silence is their only sound.

When your world starts fallin' in;
you need a chance to start again
I'll be there at your command,
I will always be your man.

Just keep holdin' on.
You know I will come along.
Just keep holdin' on.
Together we'll sing
a sweet love song.

Faces of Freedom

It was Willie and Moe in Greycliff, Montana.
And when I stopped to ask them folks—
Won't you tell me where you're bound?
They said—Sir, we're headed east on these Eagles
from Spokane, Washington, to Milwaukee town.

Headed to the Harley celebration!

As I watched them roll away on them Eagles
I remember reachin' skyward with both hands
and I thanked my lucky stars and the good Lord up above
just for givin' me the chance to live in this great land

where we've got freedom, freedom, freedom.
Our forefathers gave us sweet freedom.

I met Evangelina down in West Yellowstone.
She had moved up from south Texas,
though she had to move alone.
She'd grown weary of a man
tryin' to crush her with his hands.
Now she's waitin' on tables and workin' on her own
kind of freedom, freedom, freedom.
She's workin' on her own kind of freedom.

There were buffaloes grazin' in them big green valleys.
And I watched eagles soarin' in them big blue skies.
They love freedom, freedom, freedom.
Give them freedom—sweet, sweet freedom.

Then I met my new friend, Joe, on that Crowe reservation
and we walked into his teepee and we talked about our ways.
Talked of love and peace and beauty and truth and understandin',
and we vowed to push for freedom for the rest of our days.

Gonna push for freedom, freedom, freedom.
Brothers and sisters, come on! Push for freedom.

As I rolled into Dakota I looked up into them hills
and the faces that I saw there they ride my memory still.
There was Washington, Jefferson, Roosevelt and Lincoln.
Then I saw Willie and Moe, Evangelina and Joe
with their beautiful faces of freedom—
Beautiful faces of freedom.

Brothers and sisters, you've got faces of freedom—
Beautiful faces of freedom—
Beautiful faces of freedom.